CYCLE OF DREAMS

Before you start to read this book, take this moment to think about making a donation to punctum books, an independent non-profit press,

@ https://punctumbooks.com/support/

If you're reading the e-book, you can click on the image below to go directly to our donations site. Any amount, no matter the size, is appreciated and will help us to keep our ship of fools afloat. Contributions from dedicated readers will also help us to keep our commons open and to cultivate new work that can't find a welcoming port elsewhere. Our adventure is not possible without your support.

Vive la Open Access.

Fig. 1. Detail from Hieronymus Bosch, *Ship of Fools* (1490–1500)

CYCLE OF DREAMS. Copyright © 2024 by Eric Weiskott. This work carries a Creative Commons BY-NC-SA 4.0 International license, which means that you are free to copy and redistribute the material in any medium or format, and you may also remix, transform, and build upon the material, as long as you clearly attribute the work to the author (but not in a way that suggests the author or punctum books endorses you and your work), you do not use this work for commercial gain in any form whatsoever, and that for any remixing and transformation, you distribute your rebuild under the same license. http://creativecommons.org/licenses/by-nc-sa/4.0/

First published in 2024 by dead letter office, BABEL Working Group, an imprint of punctum books, Earth, Milky Way.
https://punctumbooks.com

The BABEL Working Group is a collective and desiring-assemblage of scholar–vagabonds with no leaders or followers, no top and no bottom, and only a middle. BABEL roams and stalks the ruins of the post-historical university as a multiplicity, a pack, looking for other roaming packs with which to cohabit and build temporary shelters for intellectual vagabonds. BABEL is an experiment in ephemerality. Find us if you can.

ISBN-13: 978-1-68571-252-5 (print)
ISBN-13: 978-1-68571-253-2 (ePDF)

DOI: 10.53288/0524.1.00

LCCN: 2024947207
Library of Congress Cataloging Data is available from the Library of Congress

Editing: Vincent W.J. van Gerven Oei and SAJ
Book design: Hatim Eujayl
Cover design: Vincent W.J. van Gerven Oei

spontaneous acts of scholarly combustion

HIC SVNT MONSTRA

CYCLE OF DREAMS

Eric Weiskott

p.

Contents

Cycle of Dreams · 15

Prologue to a Vision · 23

Storm Window · 69

Inner Dream · 75

Body as Eschaton · 105

Glossary · 109
Notes · 111
Oneirography · 115

Acknowledgments

Slivers, skeletons, and early versions of these poems appeared in the following magazines:

— *Canopic Jar*: "Body as Eschaton" [early version]
— *Cricket Online Review*: "L—— Takes a Long, Long Walk," "L—— Visits the Ocean and Nearly Has an Epiphany"
— *Inverted Syntax*: "Body as Eschaton" [rewritten version]
— *Moria*: "The End" ["Nature is dead. We"]
— *The Onion Union*: bits of "Storm Window"
— *Paper Nautilus*: bits of "Storm Window"
— *SUB-LIT*: "The End" ["The moonshine hiccups"], "The End" ["We are home sometimes in autumn"], "The End" ["We all die sometimes"], "The End" ["The grapes hang like rats"]
— *Texas Review*: "Forecast"

Shorter versions of the poems entitled "The End" appeared together in my first chapbook, *Sharp Fish* (Middletown: Samizdat, 2008).

Special thanks to Elizabeth Willis, who introduced me to the field of contemporary poetry. Other creative writing comrades on the long road from Long Island to Massachusetts have been Allison Adair, Chris Boucher, Thomas Crofts, Sarah Ehrich, Edgar Garcia, Andrew Gorin, Dave Gorin, Davy Knittle, and Angie Muir.

Thanks to those who taught me how to read *Piers Plowman*: (*viva voce*) Ian Cornelius and (through their books) Ralph

Hanna, Emily Steiner, and the late Derek Pearsall. And to Roberta Frank, who taught me Old English poetry, my first area of focus and the shadow poetry of this book.

To Vincent W.J. van Gerven Oei and Eileen A. Fradenburg Joy, thank you for believing in this book.

Love and gratitude to Lili, Theo, Mom, Dad, Carl, Lisa, and George. Sofia, this book is for you.

It is like reading a commentary on an unknown text.

—Morton W. Bloomfield

CYCLE OF DREAMS

Into the unknown,
    the natural light
        between sheep and sheep
    between sheep and wolf,
sinuous, enfolding
    the sheep and the wolf.
        The natural life
    of light: to issue
and issue, unknown,   *wave or particle*
    in the presence.

In the presence
    of the dream self
        and light of the dream,
    I read an unknown
text. It is sinuous.
    It is inscribed on   *scraped, stretched skin of calf or sheep*
        or it is folded
    or it is crossed out.
It is torn in two.
    The text starts again

and it starts again:
    the unknown life.   *cycle or journey*
        An enfolding text
    A crossed-out nature
drifts through the presence
    between sheep and wolf
        between dream and dream
    between self and self.
To issue and issue,
    like commentary.

CYCLE OF DREAMS

Like commentary
    on an unknown text,
        I wake up, torn in two.
       I drift back to sleep   *uniquely among medieval dream visions*
between page and dream,
    unknown, enfolding
        the page and the dream.
    To issue in a dream
To issue in a life,
    into the present.

Only one contemporary document records the name of the poem's author.

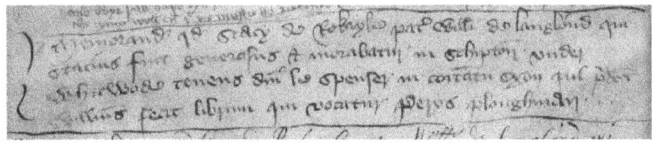

Memorandum: Eustace de Rokele was the father of William Langland; the which Eustace was of noble birth and lived in Shipton-under-Wychwood, being a tenant of Lord Despenser in Oxfordshire; the which aforesaid William made the book that is called "_____".

It sounds even more formal in Latin. The memorandum writer's primary interest was in the poet's father, Rokele. Why does Langland not share his surname? Illegitimate birth, disinheritance, a nickname, or a pseudonym are all possibilities. They all fit the poem, a cycle of dream visions whose voices of reproof spare no one, least of all the author, and whose sinuous thought evades classification. The poem oscillates between the countryside and the city (London). Langland is of two minds about everything. He represents himself as a seeker of truth and a wolf in sheep's clothing; a vagrant and a learned man with powerful friends; a radical and a reactionary; a husband and a lecher; a fraud and a prophet.

The Latin word translated as "made" is fecit, *from* facere, *the verb that gives English "artifact," "confect," and "fact."*

The Wychwoods Local History Society in nearby Milton-under-Wychwood makes no mention. The Wychwoods would claim Langland, if there was money or glory in it. "_____" stopped being a bestseller in the sixteenth century. Scholarly acceptance of Langland's authorship is a relatively recent development. "If we retain the name of Langland" for the poet, wrote the prolific editor Walter W. Skeat in 1869, "we do so chiefly for convenience." The poem engulfs even its own author.

Shipton-under-Wychwood represents, at best, a fact about a poet who lived more vividly in dreams within dreams than in the dry prose of a memorandum, where sons must stand in their fathers' shadows. Which is the real voice, the one used in life or the one used in poetry? Vision is what comes through the composition process, not before. Langland revised his poem repeatedly in the 1370s and 1380s, turning it into a commentary on itself. Historical references come unstuck from their referents. The poem overruns the moment and discovers itself, its particular undulations. The things around it soften. St. Mary's parish church in Shipton-under-Wychwood has a fifteenth-century pulpit and a thirteenth-century tower. The rectory dates from the nineteenth century.

The poem's form is antithetical to that of a memorandum. Langland's strategy is to lift you twenty feet off the ground and make you believe for one precious instant that you will not come crashing back down along with everything else. His poem enfolds the whole world, human and animal, in its oscillations. If a memorandum is gravity, "_____" is light.

PROLOGUE TO A VISION

CYCLE OF DREAMS

Here the Wanderer Lapses into a Wondrous Dream

In summertime when sunshine sing
I made a poem of my habit

addressed the wandering problem
in sheep's clothing, wondered the world

One morning near Heartbreak Hill
a *ferly* befell me, shot like magic

sick of wandering I rested there
myself by the bank of the Charles

and as I sat and heard the waters   *Long Island Sound 1986*
their sweet song swayed me to sleep

Historical Method

Don't blame the soup on the ladle. A film conceals
distance deep in our forties. The field offers

a last texture between farming and gathering.   *10,000 BC in*
Where do you go if things soften? Even April   *some places*

may be seen, cruelest month, to shimmer somewhat
in passing. History devours certificates.

Parts of us descend—
a Roman nose, a Jewish nose, out to lunch.

A person orders decaf as if to say
I own stuff too. The sheriffs rise from their desks,

called to one last non-situation.
History polices the present tense.

For *wandering,* read *vagrant.*
X marks the plot: the unknown life.

We want an imaginary bomb with real shrapnel.
We want the poem to decapitate the archbishop and the
    treasurer

in the year 1381. In the year 1986. In the year 2024.
Next year.

We want to write novels. We demand constellate history,
    daisies
shaking by the shore. Where did you go, bright friend?

I looked in history.

CYCLE OF DREAMS

Here the Dreamer

I began to dream a big dream
I was in a wilderness somewhere

and looking out toward the sun
I saw a tower made of truth

lower beneath it a prison *microcosm of a perfect society*
barbed-wired and dreadful to look at

and in between, a field of people
of all kinds of people, poor, rich
working and wandering the earth

Public Address

Stripes dines with stripes, as if intimacy
were a civic virtue.

Self-justified political inertia
for president.

In the long run, the good friends
bear themselves out: constellation

of dandies, jurors, insurgents.
Where did you go, comrades?

A committee will convene to determine
which faction has the rightful claim.

Racism is often thought to exist.
In this paper, we offer a simpler explanation.

Somewhere along the 1400 block going west, it happens:
renaissance.

Can you hear me now? screams Columbus
from the bottom of the river, petrified.

Don't ask what your country can do for you
and don't tell.

In place of a budget, a way of life.
A dress becomes a nation

through the deletion of one letter. *inflection reveals that the*
(I love that, but I also hate it.) *speaker is a woman*

PROLOGUE TO A VISION

The war was canceled at the last minute,
triggering a different war. That one will take years.   *2003–*

Learned ignorance: it takes years
to be this stupid.

Luminous darkness for Congress.
Tablets shipped to all my worshippers.

For *poetry,* read *God.* For *lyric,* read *the divine.*
For *field,* read *world.*

For *book,* read *boom.* Then: boom,
I ran out of the cave into a much bigger cave, screaming.

A golden and gleaming poetry is all too likely.
A poetry enraged, cursing, and drunk might have greater
    power.

Everything is denied and nothing is abandoned.
We appreciate your cooperation in this matter.

Here the Dreamer Sees a Latticework Containing Persons

Some put to the plow and not playing
sweated over the sowing
mass production for mass consumption

and some put to pride, dressed like pride
walked up disguised in clothing

many put to thoughts and prayers   *4% of the world's population*
lived hard for love of the Lord

in hope of an eternal life
they hole up in their cells, venture   *22% of the world's prisoners*

no joyriding in the country
even after they're paroled

Exegesis

No one understands God. All have
turned away, together, useless
and correct, administrators
of heat. Theologians make the
best atheists. I cross myself   *awkward reception after*
and then I double-cross myself.   *my bar mitzvah*
Luminous darkness, meet my fist.
Fist, meet face, chest, shoulder, shoulder.

When I was a bachelor
I spoke as a bachelor, that was
that, now is the time, in each yard
a different crism, my Jewish
savior meets Roman hands. Europe   *first use of the word*
in a word. Word, meet flesh.   *"literalism" 1644*

Here Various Employments

And some chose business (a better *productivity–pay gap*
as it might seem to our vision) *1970–*

and some toted a chirpy poem
and sang for their supper I guess

but the jokers and gossip hounds
trick up illusion, fool themselves first
trap able bodies in a book

(the preacher downtown preaches
of their tired *turpiloquium*

9-to-5 Griddle

A sorry zone ejects its employees –2019
the day *it* surfs *you,* what you are in for
my darling, the day it "organizes"
or gives or delegates the next grim world.
What is a BUSYNESS REPLY? See attachment.
Flounders man the starboard cubicle,
the pedal depresses itself, and the horn
speaks up less often. Oh the hurriednesses

of damp August! Whatever you don't do
make damned sure. The cutest little evite
even wants your garbage reply again
but you've always already "attended," *2020*
so don't leave your armchair, or whatever *from the Italian*
greater home front that now may be. *for "forty days"*

Allegory of Corporate Personhood

Corporations panhandled publicly
crammed it into bags and bellies

lied for their supper, squabbling
lord knows at the bar
                          slept with Gluttony
woke up with curses in their mouths
pursued by sleep and indolence

F

A stellar fuck-all of pronouns
invests literature.   *MFA vs. NYC*

An imaginary bomb comes for the archbishop.
Poetry is destructive, but history is creative.

The stakes are so high because the stakes are so low.

This poem has a body count.
"This poem has a body count."

The streets are gunked and dangerous
and the ones buried above them.

No one can thrive at this altitude.

Every unhappy
realization is unhappy

in its own way. Warily, Tolstoy
lowers the quotation marks

and fades into the cartoon hedge.

The barber wields decades, decades
belong to this season's haircut.

This time, I'd like you to cut it   *an as yet unknown,*
in the shape of capitalism.   *but profound, geometry*

Please. I'm begging you.

Get a haircut or we'll buy you out.
That does it! Pierces the stale

heavy air of the boardroom
or the oak-paneled seminar room

the red thunderous F.

The Dreamer Regards Ones Lately Returned from the Holy Land

Travelers and tourists struck a deal
to visit the Grand Old World

headed out to the usual spots
free to lie about it after

I saw some who claimed they found selves
every tale false in its own way
the tongue false within the trip *can't go home again*

Unfinished Country

Even the stars up here look like a mess.
It is calm, disgusts everyone, there are
many things nearby being eaten, plants
participate. Nothing happens, there's no map,
we are no cowboys, we have no heroes
among us, here we are, we are painfully
visible. There is no harmony
in the universe but invisible

harmony. History stops whirring   *has never been actualized*
while we consider ourselves, our standing,
what we want. The idea of Africa
sells some books. We die seriatim, far
from God, the treetrunks resemble scowls,
we give up all hope, and it starts again.

CYCLE OF DREAMS

Time of Pestilence

A bunch of televangelists
to New Haven and their hookers, too   *I-91 bisects I-95*

big lubbers too lazy to work
bought slim white linen suits and shirts
passed themselves off as visionaries

I found anchors from all the networks
preaching to people for profit

glossed the globe however they liked
dressed it in Gucci / Gulf / Goldman

(many of them live in costume
money sewn into their business

ever since the coming of plague
wonders have been much witnessed

if they don't hold with honest work
the end of the word draweth nigh

Forecast

After the season of snow comes the snow season, dragging
winter 2014/15
across the mountain passes and gas stations like the pad of a
hand, flexing
outward from North America with its finger on North Dakota,
eating
its words like an ambitious weatherman. After the snow season,
I rambled through the slush from Massachusetts to
Massachusetts,
slogan to slogan, newly employed. The president hasn't been to
my Massachussetts,
or yours, either, but he owns the brochure. The road to Montreal
is paved with good inventions, smartphone to smartphone, but
billboards
are prohibited in Vermont. After the season of snow
comes the snow season, and after the snow season I give up
my license and registration, my rights and appurtenances.
    Zones
coincide with other zones. Notice the dream self frozen on the
sidewalk.
    The end of the world as we know it leaves us cold, then
hot as hell.   *2016*
    We turn away for one goddamn century and look what
happens.

Here the Poet Addresses You

A loan shark preached there like a boss
fumbled out a contract under seal

and said he could absolve them all
of street hunger and broken vows

idiots liked the cut of his contract
knelt down to kiss it in alleys

and he smacked them with the letter
and collected on his own lie

(thus you bankroll charlatans
and pad pockets of corruption

if the mayor were worth a damn
the city seal would mean something

but the mayor didn't force him
the beat cop and the loan shark split   *ACAB*
fifty–fifty the gotten gains

Sonnet for All the Readers Out There

I no longer believe in the reincarnation
of your boot-soles. Are you nervous?
Stimulation and depression don't cancel each other out.
Excellence in the form of repetition.
This letter may come as a surprise to you
since we do not know each other personally.
This one goes out to all my recipients.
No longer lives at this address.
Highway collision through the eyes of the deer.
The president declares war on abstraction. Proof
is in the morning. This is practice.
A book in the raw. *Durable thing*
    I thought I understood.
    Then things came clear to you, and I lost it.

A Litany of Perversions of the Body Politic

Bosses complained to City Hall
their people were poor since 2008

asked for kickbacks for city
construction and police overtime

reps and DAs, white and half-white
who wear the city seal to say

"I write the checks that pay the rent
preach honest work and feed the poor"
laze around downtown on Mondays

some serve on the county court
and take bribes to sink hard cases
and evict "losers and creeps" *2,348 living on the street 2019*

and some land sweet private contracts
for lords and ladies of Brookline

shirk their cases, petitions
rot in the inbox
               watch out for
the big appeals court in the sky

The Fall

The hackneyed metaphor acquires a comic truth
and the truth acquires symbolic depth.
Dreaming that you woke up is not the same as
waking up in a dream.
For example:
The appletrees thunder out plums and pears.
Fool yourself first. Observance teeters
too quickly to notice. Wolves eat sheep
and we eat sheep. Grim turn for the farm.
This autumn, let's try something new.
The swine begin an all-pearls diet
without hunger, joy, or gratitude.
> Dogs used to eat anything red
> but they have asked, and we have given.

Here the Dreamer Implicates Himself in the Vision

I saw the power of college   *Middletown, CT 2005–2009*
to open the door and shut it

education: a form of love
in seven forms, the liberal arts

that live in departments, the gates
to every heavenly suburb
opened for them and closed again

but the deanlets and vice provosts
who presumed to pay teachers
to wield that power
              —I won't bash
since education pays my rent   *15% below or near*
I can and can't speak of provosts   *the poverty line*

From Scratch

To make an apple pie from scratch,
first invent the universe.

A lunch pierces an era.
See, this is not what I was taught

at all, the universe hurtles, *has a finite velocity*
appears elsewhere, brave and clueless.

We are mostly scratch, equations
soften, this isn't the house

in the catalogue, just bring me
coffee! They offer three sizes

past large, miscommunication
begins as planned, five o' clock, give

and give again. Einstein at work,
Einstein on the toilet, Einstein

with bowl of fruit, crowds of people *limits the speed*
furious, smiling, furious, *of our perceptions*

young, having proven nothing.

Here a Political World Materializes

Then came there a brave President
and power to the People

and Common Sense and his pundits
came to advise the President

the President with Common Sense
set the People to feed themselves

the People had Common Sense too
and organized into communes   *posture that politics is*
to sow the word and reap the text   *just posture*

President, People, Common Sense
made law and justice, tooth and nail

Even Nostalgia Must Be Learned

Even nostalgia must be learned
    like a dumb tourniquet, always
        way too late. Reader, have you
    noticed the way the weeks furrow

together, Wednesday to Wednesday,
    all the same temperature?
        The "Worst President" stickers
    campaign again, "it's common sense,"

and deer prepare for winter.
    It is a pretty foolish winter,
        too, reader, fancying itself
    a kind of preliminary

but indispensable test
    for a future we'd rather not
        inhabit unconditionally.
    Common sense for president.   *Four. More. Years.*

Give and take, or give and give.
    Speech is like that, full of ringing
        vowels and blunted vowels.
    The buzzword has grown a pair.

It was not so long ago that
    I parleyed with you, my friend:
        we two memorandum'd our way
    to oblivion, only survived

by a few notes, which see below,
    reader, the very matter at
        heart. It is a crafty liar
    who, loved or hated, obliges

a literate citizenry.
>He's holed up in his old haunts,
>>refusing the moment, faking
>the hottest first term on record.

Here the Dreamer Witnesses an Instructional Scene

Then a lunatic took the floor
and kneeling said knowingly

"God bless you, Mr. President
and may you lead us loyally
and rewarded be your government"

And then an angel from above
condescended in Latin
          so
the people could be justified
in taking it anymore

                    the angel said
"First world and free world" Neither, soon!
Oh Commander in Chief,
do well and be more good than fair
and clothe the naked Lady Law

What you sow, that shall you reapen
naked law judges nakedly
sow good will and reap good press

Then a glutton of words spoke up   *wandering satirist*
answering the angel on high

Since a Pre-si-dent presides,
the name without the man decides

Then all the people cried in Latin
prostrate (translate if you can)

Novus ordo seculorum

From Above

Thursday is tomorrow again. I have forgotten
people's faces and if it is polite

or it is not polite. It is as if a star
no one has named,

somewhere in our own universe,
because we have the wrong instruments for looking.

In caves along the river, Plato's
prisoners wave the figurines

I have sent away for with
nineteen box tops.

Sometimes the darkness shines.
Sometimes it's just darkness.

The news is always one incubation period too late.

I have forgotten Tuesday and some
concert venues there. As if from around corners,

from underneath boxes in offices,
when brightness intercedes.

Here we are, chained in the reading room
with the other books.

I saved up for this one for weeks.
When the package arrived, I felt immediate disappointment.

I used to hate running in it.
Now, I never notice.

Distancing guidelines are subject to change
in light of new observations.

When you are inside it, it appears to be expanding.
From above, all curves are flat. *wave or particle*

Luminous darkness, and we're here all week.

An Interlude in the Same Key

Just then a bunch of rats and mice
ran out, a thousand or so

called a council for the people
because a cat came sometimes

and pounced on them and snatched them up
and battered them like pincushions

"We're terrified to leave the house
and if we complain, he'll scratch us

and put us under his thumb
until we wish we were dead

if we could ever resist him
we would be lords of our domain"

A Thing That Moves in All Directions at Once

A thing that moves in all directions at once *there is*
stands on each corner like rainwater *no outside*
loads a pistol in any window
leaves each of us smoking in the bed
buys up our childhood homes
gives our mothers the pink slip
leverages innovative rodent solutions
speaks up against integrating our schools
is felt but is not seen
is felt but is not mentioned in high school history
   textbooks *perhaps cannot be actualized*
is felt but is not regulated by law
is felt but is not a concern among a majority of Americans
   according to a recent poll.
     A thing that wrecks the air like butterflies:
     the unspeakably beautiful violence of our lives.

Here Language Betrays Action

A famous fellow traveler
suggested counter-surveillance

"I've seen people up in Cambridge
wear bright bangles around their necks
and ornate collars
                       they walked unleashed
in the suburbs, wherever they pleased,
parks and offices as I hear

with a bell attached, seems to me
you'd know where they went and could hide

thusly" (said the rat) "it makes sense
we buy a brass or silver bell

and loop it onto a collar
and hang it on the cat's neck

then we'd hear where he went
and if he came in peace, we'd look
him in the eye
                       otherwise
if he's hunting we'd run away"

The rodent parliament concurred
but when they bought the bell and collar

there was no rat in the lot of them
who dared to tie it on the cat
not for dollar pound or yuan

realized they were chicken, plan shot
their labor lost, their learning lost

Transcript

When we are talking about war
we are really talking about
peace, our secret peace button,
our peace machine. Here they give you
a place to sleep, square meals, movie
money. We live on happiness.
We send our children, it is bright
every day, the heads in our screens,
the digital eyelid flutters
more than realistically, "captures"
my "heart." We are really talking.
A peace transacted by drone strikes.
    A series of the mildest day
      recorded.

CYCLE OF DREAMS

Here the Interlude Draws to a Point

A party loyalist stood forth
(as I dreamed) and in their presence
addressed these words to the senate

"Even if we kill him, there'll be
more domestic terrorists

so my advice is leave him be
and hope he never sees the bell

rabbiting he'll pass over us
praise be to his lamb dinner

papercuts sure beat a blowtorch
damned if we'll miss the odd comrade

years ago my dad used to say
'dark times when the leader's a liar'

you read the same in the news
undermining our democracy

but we deserve it anyway   *of all possible worlds*
we're the mice in the malt liquor
you rats chew through people's clothing

without the cat in office
you beasts couldn't govern your own selves

To me" (said the mouse) "it's too risky
you won't catch me inciting grief

his conscience doesn't bother me
or when it did I wouldn't shriek

Song for Pragmatic Communists

The pragmatic communist votes for the fascist.
The pragmatic communist stays home.
Pragmatism and communism have a long, untold history
and the pragmatic communist has learned to tell it.
The white domestic terrorist has composed a communist
    manifesto.
The networks have a field day. This democracy
isn't going to undermine itself. Is it?
The white domestic terrorist has composed a communist
    manifesto.
The pragmatic communist works within the system.
The pragmatic communist chips away behind the scenes.
Pragmatism is doing the same thing over and over
and expecting the same problems.
> Words bent around pain, words bent around money:
> a melancholy communism that has learned to disrupt the
> competition.

CYCLE OF DREAMS

I'd non-violently suffer him
his preferred hunting patterns
it's everyone for themselves"

Tell me the meaning of my dream
you crafty readers if you know

CYCLE OF DREAMS

The Dreamer Has a Vision of the Legal Profession

A hundred more in shark suits
lawyers and DAs barred and served

pleaded for cash and licked the law
had nothing to say on Sundays

bottle the mist out at Seaport   *I-93 buried 1991–2007*
as soon as get "mum" from them

Mimesis

Reality needs representation, fast.
I know a poet.
It is a matter of pleading your case,   *rap battles in the cafeteria*
in the process discovering the self who pleads.
It is a matter of standing.
Money speaks.
Legalis homo out for a jog.
Legalis homo with bowl of fruit.
I know a guy who knows himself.
What's legal is another story.
The poem conveys precedents
more than realistically.
    Aristotle turns in his grave   *a reform that has hitherto*
    and just like that the genre changes.   *always been lacking*

CYCLE OF DREAMS

Here the Dream Fabric Reveals a First Seam

Brahmins yuppies and other
Harvard alums I spotted too

bakers brewers butchers tailors
plumbers cashiers masons nurses

teachers nannies and janitors
many other kinds of labor

some of each stood forth in that place *detention causes*
bus drivers PAs delinquents *recidivism*
peppering the day with
        baby you know I do

sidewalk sandwich boards yelled puns *reopening for*
on pies pork DINNER SPECIAL *curbside pickup only*

bar doors with brewery stickers
Harpoon Sam Adams Allagash
Brooklyn Guinness Lagunitas

dreaming I saw this and much more

Darkly

Write it back into the book   *book of the true poem*
like a first strong midnight,
realer than portents
and felt as if from a great distance.
Put it backwards
so you can see it
    there.

STORM WINDOW

CYCLE OF DREAMS

Draw the shades. Forget
the shades.

Installation: four squares of glass,
edged with white paint. First disassemble
this room.

Exercise: imagine *which,* a grammar
of antecedence and dislocation.
Installation: shadow.

Draw the shades. Imagine fire,
rain,
lightning against the pane.

This is not rain
but the forgotten remnant of ascending sky.

Imagine light: rope stapled
at one end to surfaces.
White rope.
Gnomon of light
at sea.

Imagine red: a receding
sun against night's cool
sphygmomanometer.

When I leave this place,
remember me as the farmer
remembers the house's youth.

STORM WINDOW

Exercise: thin the walls to turpentine
transparence. The ceiling
is a roof's belly,
fat with rain.

An empty house, but in the last room
still life composed of bed things.

A sheen supplants the visible
quicker than focus.
Shock of *has been snowing:*
its drifts
beyond amount.
Snow across the sea.

Unfix a sense of color
and shadow.
Unfix material: cedar
and silver.

Imagine my window: one pane storm,
three panes ocean.

After a thunderstorm, the tall sea
glistens with underneathlessness.

CYCLE OF DREAMS

When I leave this place, forget
my shape and my possessions.

Unfix a sense of falling back to sleep
at midnight.

An empty street, but in the last backyard
to-do lists germinate.
The names of liquors and philosophers
supplant the patio:

house of the mind.

STORM WINDOW

I do not know whether it is a whale
singing or an imagined
barrier of sea
   tall
and liquid
     which
separates and
      re
distributes heaving.

In crystal blue tones it
translates *sun*.

CYCLE OF DREAMS

A model of your sleeping self arises
in a fog of pointillism.
The radio by the window frames a thunderstorm
against woods.

Nothing exists behind these plastic generals, green skies
and circuitry, a vase made more valuable
by having cracked and been repaired with gold.

Squint and this becomes the world.

Describe a signal but omit
its destination.
Light on the sea.
An arrow among cedar twigs
in high grass.
A philosopher's paradox.

When I leave this place,
remember me as wheat
remembers a particular
summer day.
A lamp twinkles in a high window
someplace, quicker than focus.

Wake up
bookended by *forget*.
Imagine
a barn thing, or a light
on someone else's waves.

INNER DREAM

Here the Dreamer Finds Religion in the Form of a Woman

I searched for meaning in the tower   *east past the end of I-495*
and the prison and the field

a beautiful woman in white
came down and called me by my name

"Are you asleep? see the people
working and wandering the earth?

most of them want nothing but cash
and no better than some respect
and no other heaven than here"

Frightened of her austere beauty
I asked, "What does it signify?"

L—— Gives You Tips on How To Deal with Negative Criticism

She also covers butterfly anatomy. Application-scope settings are read only at run time. For example, a setting that holds a user preference of color would be a System. L—— gives a variety of tips for an aspiring model seeking a reputable modeling agency or photographer. Settings have two possible scopes: application scope and user scope. The Add New Item dialog box opens. L—— explains where procrastination stems from. She also outlines what questions good breeders may ask you. For example, you might want to change a connection string to point to the correct database location. L—— covers readiness, clothing and equipment, abnormal responses, dangers, repetitive stress injuries, and more. These values are called settings. L—— provides suggestions to help re-condition the mind. How To Bathe Your Dog. How To Care for Houseplants. How To Grow Your Own Chili Peppers. Once a setting is created, it can be assessed in code using the mechanisms described later in this article. Info on surgical bra fit, maternity and nursing bra fit, too. Reduce Stress and Rebuild Connections. Although she suggests learning from a professional first, L—— gives step-by-step instructions on how to do it yourself. L—— explains what causes snoring in adults and children. How To Raise Your Self. The new value persists for the duration of the application session.

Here the Dreamer Finds Himself in a Mirror

I wept after her furious words
then drowsed until I fell asleep

I dreamed another big dream
Fortune raptured me away

into the land of unlikeness
to peer into a dark mirror

Fortune said to me, "Behold   *Early Decision applicants*
what you desire and might obtain"

L—— Takes a Long, Long Walk

The river wanders like an electronic half-penny withdrawn without notice. The forest yawns. Click here. One weird trick novelists don't want you to know about. Once even paper was considered a notable invention. Capital letters are called "upper case" because of the distribution of moveable type in drawers in early printing shops. A typist missing the *W* marshals the intermittent clamor. Shouting over the din, L—— explains how to write a novel in no time at all. Is it still a walk if you can't go home again? Is it a mirror if you can't find yourself? Years later, scholars pore over her papers, in search of. Her writing means something different now because of what it appears to have meant then. Augustine describes the visible world as the *regio dissimilitudinis,* where things are not as they seem. Dear diary: You will never guess what I did today.

Recklessness, a Poet, and a Youth

"Who cares?" laughed a reckless vagrant   *37 years old*
"Old Age is a long walk from here
hobble and scruple when you're dead"

"Man *proponit*," declaimed a poet
"and God *disponit*: truth demands

an actual response, fortune
a possible response, the flesh
an automatic response"

"Bye now!" laughed a teen and led me   *kissing in the darkness*
until all my works were carnal   *of the movie theater*

L—— Visits the Ocean and Nearly Has an Epiphany

It pummels the surf; it is not meant. It arises. So the phoenix wrangles its cracked skin, always the last time. Along the beach are cabanas, each serving the same brew. A lonely jug dribbles like a wino, but no one is there to see. See wino. L—— covers swimming, first aid, CPR, the cost of an ambulance, the cost of two nights in the intensive care unit, the address of the unemployment office, the name of a good shrink, the number of a shark of a divorce lawyer, the feeling that has been lost in these United States. Back home, it is a view you can't get. The card shark's next draw is visible to viewers of the program but not to the shark. We're going to need a bigger table. Possible response runs the table, then actual response. Pokerfaced. Stone cold. Like a rock. Like Iraq. Like a rack used for storing magazines. Like a gun stuffed in the stocking like a flounder. Fleshy and feeding on the bottom.

Discourse upon Attraction

Love is celestial remedy   *impressed everyone with our first dance*
antidote to covetous living

love is the force that overwhelmed
the ancients and filled the tablets

love is omnipotent, peaceful
so heavy that it fell to earth
and dined on the things of the world

but once incarnate, is love not
lighter than a leaf and sharper

than a needle to penetrate
any heart and every high wall?

L—— Enrolls in a Physics Class

At a molecular level, there is no cold as such. There is only attraction: a shock of ice covets me with especial zeal. Heat finds a way. Master of possession: warm cattle abroad and afoot. Cattle, whose former name means "money," "value," and "salary." An unexpected intersection between physics and animal husbandry derails our conversation nationally. Although she suggests learning from a professor first, L—— gives step-by-step instructions on how to do it from a great distance. Desire, writes Anne Carson, is about the impossible transcendence of the self. The ice has no inner space, nor do warmer animals refuse us.

CYCLE OF DREAMS

Discoursing with Himself, the Dreamer Passes into Another Dream

So I wandered in sheep's clothing
in a wilderness somewhere

melodious birds overhead
I sat a while beneath an elm *had seasonal allergies*
listened to their desirous hymns *for the first time*

their sweet song swayed me to sleep
I dreamed another big dream
bigger than a country, I thought

One who looked exactly like me
came up and called me by my name

"Who are you? how do you know my name?"
"You already know the answer"

"I do?"
    "Don't you know who I am?
haven't you seen me pursuing you
for seven years?"

The End

The moonshine hiccups
and it is July everywhere

as if certain elms stood for us,
smoking somewhere in Morse code   *on and off*

and they have fallen
for the first time:

as if *bad* explodes
and we are children again, in our own   *minds*
countries, envelopes of ache.

We did our best thinking
under threat of reaching the end of things.

We created a secret language
then forgot it.

We had summers off.

We broke our bottles everywhere,
damned and okay.

The Tree of Imaginable Virtue in the Orchard of the Body

"Envision love as a tall tree
the roots, mercy; the trunk, pity

the leaves are true words and the law
the blossoms are lovers' secrets

the tree is known as patience
and the fruit is unbending love"

"I would travel miles to see it
and eat the apples off the branch   *the reach*
tell me where I can find this tree"

"The orchard where it grows is in
the human body: the roots stick

in the human heart, and the one
who tends to the tree is desire
working under P———"

"P———!" in rapturous joy
at hearing the name, I fainted

and I had another vision
I thought I saw P——— there

in the orchard, showing me the tree
and what was supporting the tree

The End

We are home sometimes in autumn,
out past the orchard.

All our desires have spoiled.
All our sentences have been served.

TIME TO GO
the sunshine sing.

How strange to reach the end anywhere
after a lifetime of reaching.

Here the Dreamer Comes To Understand the Law of Opposite Forces

Soon enough I was dreaming
that my enemy in the form

of a man ripped out the truth
and he shook it by the roots

fiction and falsehood sprang out there
in each country as he advanced *my own worst enemy*
he cultivated treachery

The End

This is a year of green phenomena:

the apples turn bad from all corners.
The ocean lawyers the land.

The sky indicts
the green earth.

Fiction is a life lived on false pretenses
known to everyone.

Truth is an indescribable life
lived by a hidden principle.

This is the end, now.

The soil bears witness
but the forests recant.

A Vast, Composite Mirror of Many Polished Surfaces

I gazed at the sea and the stars
saw unaccountable wonders

flowers in the forests, blue and   *trail around Inlet Pond*
white and purple in the green grass

sour and sweet and all marvelous
indescribably numerous

What moved me the most was seeing
how order ruled the natural world
of animals
               —except for us
who, rich and poor, lived in disorder

so I challenged Order and asked
"If you're so smart, why don't you rule
humankind like the animals?"

Order rebuked me: "Don't worry
if I don't; it's not your concern
fix it yourself"

The End

Well, biologists,
your bottled lizards filled the books.

Then the books burned
and we had to rewrite them,

which we did, with immense sadness
and a series of educated guesses.

This is a year of crazy searching:

we rebuild our temples
and investigate our own case.

Above the country   *a T inside an O: Africa, Asia, Europe*
and the map of it,

an o of rain. But who looks
upward from any yard now?

Here we are, even history is here,
the very last fool under the tiered skies.

Here the Dreamer Witnesses the Crucifixion

A thief gazed out on PAY IT BACK
despaired because he had nothing

softly he said to just himself
"Jesus, who died upon the cross

when a thief asked for forgiveness
you thought to have mercy on him

have mercy on me who can't pay
and has no hope of earning it

I ask you to be good, not fair
don't account ill of me at the end"

I can't say what became of him

The End

Upon the T of the gas station logo,
hungry Jesuses bicker.

In place of a foreign policy,
a crude, viscous liquid.

We use one pronoun for invasions   *and another for*
and another for trade agreements.   *unpublished drone strikes*

Our cities reflect our buried dreams
of a future adequate to the present tense.

The neighborhood is divided in the abstract
and then concretely.

This is the end of our dispute,
one way or the other.

Please hold.

Our cars wait in line out of habit,
digital or not.

CYCLE OF DREAMS

Text for an Unimagined Commentary

and I woke up and wrote my dream   *a file that was never closed*

The End

Is this the right place,
types the wolf, the moon *in so many poems*
is right there, is this
it?

Commentary on an Unseen Text

A professor offered to read it *my parents' tattered copy*
and render it in plain English *summer after high school*

P—— unfolded the text
and I peered over his shoulder

the text was simple, just two lines
inscribed in true characters—

[[
       ]   ]

The professor became confused
and issued a commentary

"a search for truth, love, and justice *$[ ]1,000 per year*
in an intolerable world" *plus benefits*

P—— tore the text in two
in righteous fury

The End

Here are people in actual places
praying and searching,

here we are, dreams and all,
in the streets.

If you lived here, you'd be home now.
We are here to protest the conditions

governing our consent,
and we are here in spirit,

and we are only here for the weekend,
and we are not here for that.

The protester becomes a statistic
and statistics become a form of prayer
and prayer becomes a form of protest.

The quarterback kneels a decade early
and four centuries after the fact.   *2016–1619*

This is a year of buried ledes
that stay buried.

Here Time Irradiates the Dreamer All at Once

"Now I see," said Life, "medicine
is no match for creeping old age"

and Life bucked up and drove onward
to a drunken celebration   *beer special at Gryphon's Pub*
"comfort in human company"

but Old Age drove after him   *time penetrates the body*
zoomed over the crown of my head
leaving me permanently bald

"Stupid Old Age," I said, "piss off!
since when was my head a highway?
at least you could have asked nicely"

"Nicely?" he sneered, and laced into me
he boxed my ears and made me deaf

he slugged me, knocking out my teeth   *tore through Suffolk*
he imprisoned me with frailty   *County's nursing homes*

my wife began to pity me
and wish I were dead already

the part of me she loved to feel
at night when we were by ourselves

—I couldn't get it up for her
because Old Age had beaten it down

The End

We all die sometimes,
quoting Tennyson or baking, *here lies one*
engraven on the day.

One pronoun for the living and another for the departed.

When I died, my future
flashed before my eyes.

I thought, there has been some mistake.
I'd like to speak to the manager.

We did our best dying under threat of *shrapnel*
living to fight another day.

What fancy flour
what wonky commies
at last, life on the bomb.

And we all think, *to have loved and lost.*

Here a Congregation Forms

In my immense sadness I saw *regret to inform you*
the death of nature, and death came

for me: I cried out to Nature
"Old Age has paid me a visit
avenge me when I leave this place"

"Go into the barn Unity *importance of academic "pedigree"*
and stay until I send for you
but learn some art before you do"

"Tell me, which art should I learn?"
"The art of love, and no other"

"But isn't the job market bad?"
"Love well," said Nature, "and you'll have
always a roof over your head"

And so I began to wander

The End

Nature is dead. We
represent ourselves

in love, late for work,
charged with foolishness.

In place of nature, a coin-operated binocular.
In place of history, a dissertation.

The parts of this book:

De miseria humane nature
De mundo et delicijs eius   *diesel smell in the*
De morte et quid est mors.   *barn my father built*

What large cars we make each spring,
stuffed with love letters to the living.

The present mass-produces the future tense.
We congregate.

Here the Vision Attains Its Analeptic Ending

Conscience cried out, "I will wander
in the wilderness of this world

I'll go in search of P——
who can deliver justice for all

Nature, avenge me now and send
strength until I find P——"

he said much more, but I woke up

The End

The grapes hang like rats
fanged, unwilling,

a new wine, angry
and real.

This is a year of endings
without new beginnings:

a year with only one vintage.
A world with only one pronoun,
a communism pathetic not triumphant.

When one door closes,
it's closed for good.

This is the end.
We search in the barns
and sleep in the barns.

BODY AS ESCHATON

CYCLE OF DREAMS

Tree in lagoon,
                  body as eschaton:
                  a limit named epidermis,
the prolepsis of root.

Call it swamp, but the tree
has no root.

                  First remember the body's
                  places: the places *for* not *of*
                  the body you inhabit.
                  Both *place* and *reemerge*.

The surface of the water
admits no depth.

                  Body as clock: first forget
                  sleep and other absences
                  of the body from time. Remember
                  times of action in sequence
                  or in alternation. Times of *same*.

Sunshine.

                  Next delete etymology:
                  a whiteness of symbols.

Nearby stands an angular
stone complex. Dusk.
Squat tree.

                  The body reemerges
                  as its own horizon, its
                  own sex, its power. Body
                  as phoenix: exert the body.

Wind avoids this place.

> Build the body: pulleys, a sock, wagon, wrench,
> pushpins, microscope, shotgun,
> a socket, pen, slippers, tape,
> rope, needle, chain, gloves, mower,
> rattle, fin, latch, cars, a ring,
> nut, bat, phonograph, buckles,
> snap, cleats, a vase, machete,
> string, plates, bar, lever, doorbell.

People paddle toward the tree
mistaking it for somewhere.

> How to hold another body,
> its own sex, its power? Times
> of *same*. Is there room
> for relation? Hold the body.
> There shall be time until *forget
> its times*. Pose the body, your
> own body.

The lagoon has swallowed cars
and [list of objects].
Flat water.

> I understand your
> body through its hold on mine. Own
> your
> body, own it, immortal
> body, but not its places.

Glossary

ferly — marvel (Middle English)
novus ordo seculorum — new world order (Latin)
proponit...disponit — proposes...disposes (Latin)
regio dissimilitudinis — land of unlikeness (Latin)
turpiloquium — obscene speech (Latin)

Notes

xiii: Epigraph: Morton W. Bloomfield, *Piers Plowman as a Fourteenth-Century Apocalypse* (New Brunswick: Rutgers University Press, 1962), 32.

15: "Cycle of Dreams": The fifteenth-century manuscript with the shelfmark Dublin, Trinity College, MS 212 (translation mine); William Langland, *The Vision of William Concerning Piers the Plowman,* ed. Walter W. Skeat (Oxford: Clarendon, 1869), xiv. See Robert Adams, *Langland and the Rokele Family: The Gentry Background to* Piers Plowman (Dublin: Four Courts, 2013). The authorship question was settled by George Kane, *Piers Plowman: The Evidence for Authorship* (London: Athlone, 1965). Images: Fig. 1. Dublin, Trinity College, MS 212, folio 89v, detail; fig. 2. Church Green, Shipton-under-Wychwood, Oxfordshire (photo credit: A. Sofia Warner).

23: The poems on the versos are very loosely adapted from the complete text of the prologue and select later passages of the second or "B" version of William Langland's *Piers Plowman. Piers Plowman* is an enigmatic alliterative poem written in the wake of the waves of bubonic plague in England in 1348 and 1361–1362. Langland mounts a search for truth, love, and justice in an intolerable world. Uniquely among medieval dream visions, the poem describes a cycle of dreams. "P——" corresponds to the elusive title character, Piers the plowman.

25: "Historical Method": T.S. Eliot, *The Waste Land* (New York: Boni & Liveright, 1922), 9, and Ben Lerner, *The Hatred of Poetry* (New York: Farrar, Straus & Giroux, 2016), 39.

26: "Here the Dreamer," gloss: Michel Foucault, *Discipline and Punish: The Birth of the Prison,* trans. Alan Sheridan (New York: Vintage, 1977), 238.

27: "Public Address": *Wulf and Eadwacer,* l. 12; Denys Turner, *The Darkness of God: Negativity in Christian Mysticism* (Cambridge: Cambridge University Press, 1995), 22, 25, and 272. For *Wulf and Eadwacer,* see George Philip Krapp and Elliott Van Kirk Dobbie, eds., *The Exeter Book* (New York: Columbia University Press, 1936).

31: "Exegesis": The fragmentary fifth-century Gothic text known as *Skeireins (Explanation),* a commentary on the gospel of John. Gloss: John Milton, *Doctrine and Discipline of Divorce,* 2nd edn. (London, 1644).

35: "F": Lev N. Tolstoy, *Anna Karenina* (Moscow: Ris, 1878). Gloss: Foucault, *Discipline and Punish,* 316n12.

39: "Unfinished Country": Werner Herzog in Les Blank, dir., *Burden of Dreams* (1982), and Heraclitus, *Fragments,* trans. Brooks Haxton (New York: Penguin, 2001), fr. 47.

43: "Sonnet for All the Readers Out There," gloss: Elizabeth Willis, *Turneresque* (Providence: Burning Deck, 2003), 42.

44: "A Litany of Perversions of the Body Politic," gloss: Arianna MacNeill, "The City Took Its Annual Homeless Census Wednesday Night. Here's What to Know," *boston.*

com, January 30, 2020, https://www.boston.com/news/local-news/2020/01/30/annual-boston-homeless-census-2020/.

45: "The Fall": Robert Worth Frank, Jr., *Chaucer and* The Legend of Good Women (Cambridge: Harvard University Press, 1972), 22.

47: "From Scratch": Carl Sagan in TV series *Cosmos* (1980). Gloss: George Kubler, *The Shape of Time: Remarks on the History of Things* (New Haven: Yale University Press, 1962), 18.

57: "A Thing That Moves in All Directions at Once," gloss: Foucault, *Discipline and Punish*, 301.

59: "Transcript": "President George W. Bush Speaks to HUD Employees on National Homeownership Month," *U.S. Department of Housing and Urban Development (HUD)*, June 18, 2002, https://archives.hud.gov/remarks/martinez/speeches/presremarks.cfm.

65: "Mimesis," gloss: Foucault, *Discipline and Punish*, 270.

66: "Here the Dream Fabric Reveals a First Seam," gloss: Foucault, *Discipline and Punish*, 265.

67: "Darkly," gloss: Guillaume de Machaut, *Le livre du voir dit*.

77: "L—— Gives You Tips on How To Deal with Negative Criticism": "Using Settings in C#," *Microsoft*, February 3, 2012, https://learn.microsoft.com/en-us/previous-versions/aa730869(v=vs.80), and a series of emails sent by Boston College's Human Resources department in spring and summer 2020.

79: "L—— Takes a Long, Long Walk": Augustine of Hippo adapted the idea of the *regio dissimilitudinis* from a phrase in Plato's *Statesman*.

83: "L—— Enrolls in a Physics Class": Anne Carson, *Eros the Bittersweet: An Essay* (Princeton: Princeton University Press, 1986), 30–31. The Old English word *feoh* has the basic meaning "cattle" and the extended meanings "money," "value," and "salary."

86: "The Tree of Imaginable Virtue in the Orchard of the Body," gloss: Carson, *Eros the Bittersweet*, 26–29.

90: "A Vast, Composite Mirror of Many Polished Surfaces," title: R.F. Yeager, *John Gower's Poetic: The Search for a New Arion* (Cambridge: D.S. Brewer, 1990), 276.

94: "Text for an Unimagined Commentary," gloss: Foucault, *Discipline and Punish*, 227.

96: "Commentary on an Unseen Text": *Sir Gawain and the Green Knight*, l. 35. See Malcolm Andrew and Ronald Waldron, eds., *The Poems of the Pearl Manuscript: Pearl, Cleanness, Patience, Sir Gawain and the Green Knight*, 5th edn. (Exeter: University of Exeter Press, 2007).

98: "Here Time Irradiates the Dreamer All at Once," gloss: Foucault, *Discipline and Punish*, 152.

99: "The End": Alfred Lord Tennyson, *In Memoriam* (London: Moxon, 1850), canto 27.

101: "The End": Esaias Tegnér, "Song to the Sun" (1817), in *Anthology of Swedish Lyrics from 1750 to 1915*, trans. Charles Wharton Stork (New York: American-Scandinavian Foundation, 1917), 41; part of a fifteenth-century table of contents for the *Prick of Conscience*, a bestselling fourteenth-century English poem of religious instruction: "The misery of human nature / The world and its delights / Death and the nature of death." See Daniel Sawyer, *Reading English Verse in Manuscript, c.1350–c.1500* (Oxford: Oxford University Press, 2020). I correct "*natura*" (nominative) to "*nature*" (genitive).

Oneirography

Adams, Robert. *Langland and the Rokele Family: The Gentry Background to* Piers Plowman. Dublin: Four Courts, 2013.

Andrew, Malcolm, and Ronald Waldron, eds. *The Poems of the Pearl Manuscript: Pearl, Cleanness, Patience, Sir Gawain and the Green Knight.* 5th edn. Exeter: University of Exeter Press, 2007.

Bloomfield, Morton W. *Piers Plowman as a Fourteenth-Century Apocalypse.* New Brunswick: Rutgers University Press, 1962.

Carson, Anne. *Eros the Bittersweet: An Essay.* Princeton: Princeton University Press, 1986.

Cornelius, Ian. *Reconstructing Alliterative Verse: The Pursuit of a Medieval Meter.* Cambridge: Cambridge University Press, 2017.

Eliot, T.S. *The Waste Land.* New York: Boni & Liveright, 2022.

Foucault, Michel. *Discipline and Punish: The Birth of the Prison.* Translated by Alan Sheridan. New York: Vintage, 1977.

Frank, Robert Worth, Jr. *Chaucer and* The Legend of Good Women. Cambridge: Harvard University Press, 1972.

Frank, Roberta. *The Etiquette of Early Northern Verse.* Notre Dame: University of Notre Dame Press, 2022.

Garcia, Edgar. *Skins of Columbus: A Dream Ethnography.* Hudson: Fence, 2019.

Gruenler, Curtis A. Piers Plowman *and the Poetics of Enigma: Riddles, Rhetoric, and Theology.* Notre Dame: University of Notre Dame Press, 2017.

Hanna, Ralph. *Patient Reading / Reading Patience: Oxford Essays on Medieval English Literature.* Liverpool: Liverpool University Press, 2017.

Heraclitus. *Fragments.* Translated by Brooks Haxton. New York: Penguin, 2001.

Kane, George. Piers Plowman*: The Evidence for Authorship.* London: Athlone, 1965.

Krapp, George Philip, and Elliott Van Kirk Dobbie, eds. *The Exeter Book.* New York: Columbia University Press, 1936.

Kubler, George. *The Shape of Time: Remarks on the History of Things.* New Haven: Yale University Press, 1962.

Langland, William. *Piers Plowman: A New Annotated Edition of the C-text.* Edited by Derek Pearsall. Exeter: University of Exeter Press, 2008; repr. 2010.

———. *The Vision of Piers Plowman.* Edited by A.V.C. Schmidt. London: Everyman, 1995.

———. *The Vision of William Concerning Piers the Plowman.* Edited by Walter W. Skeat. Oxford: Clarendon, 1869.

Lerner, Ben. *The Hatred of Poetry.* New York: Farrar, Straus & Giroux, 2016.

MacNeill, Arianna. "The City Took Its Annual Homeless Census Wednesday Night. Here's What to Know." *boston.com,* January 30, 2020. https://www.boston.com/news/local-news/2020/01/30/annual-boston-homeless-census-2020/.

Milton, John. *The Doctrine and Discipline of Divorce.* 2nd edn. London, 1644.

"President George W. Bush Speaks to HUD Employees on National Homeownership Month." *U.S. Department of Housing and Urban Development (HUD),* June 18, 2002. https://archives.hud.gov/remarks/martinez/speeches/presremarks.cfm.

Sawyer, Daniel. *Reading English Verse in Manuscript, c.1350–c.1500.* Oxford: Oxford University Press, 2020.

Schlegel, Christian. *Honest James*. Northampton: Song Cave, 2015.

Steiner, Emily. *Reading* Piers Plowman. Cambridge: Cambridge University Press, 2013.

Stork, Charles Wharton, trans. *Anthology of Swedish Lyrics from 1750 to 1915*. New York: American-Scandinavian Foundation, 1917.

Tennyson, Alfred Lord. *In Memoriam*. London: Moxon, 1850.

Tolstoy, Lev N. *Anna Karenina*. Moscow: Ris, 1878.

Turner, Denys. *The Darkness of God: Negativity in Christian Mysticism*. Cambridge: Cambridge University Press, 1995.

"Using Settings in C#." *Microsoft,* February 3, 2012. https://learn.microsoft.com/en-us/previous-versions/aa730869(v=vs.80).

Willis, Elizabeth. *Turneresque*. Providence: Burning Deck, 2003.

Yeager, R.F. *John Gower's Poetic: The Search for a New Arion*. Cambridge: D.S. Brewer, 1990.

Zeeman, Nicolette. *The Arts of Disruption: Allegory and* Piers Plowman. Oxford: Oxford University Press, 2020.

www.ingramcontent.com/pod-product-compliance
Lightning Source LLC
Chambersburg PA
CBHW051132160426
43195CB00014B/2442